CITY and CHURCH in THE OLD TOWE COLORING BOOK FOR ADULTS SKETCH DESIGN

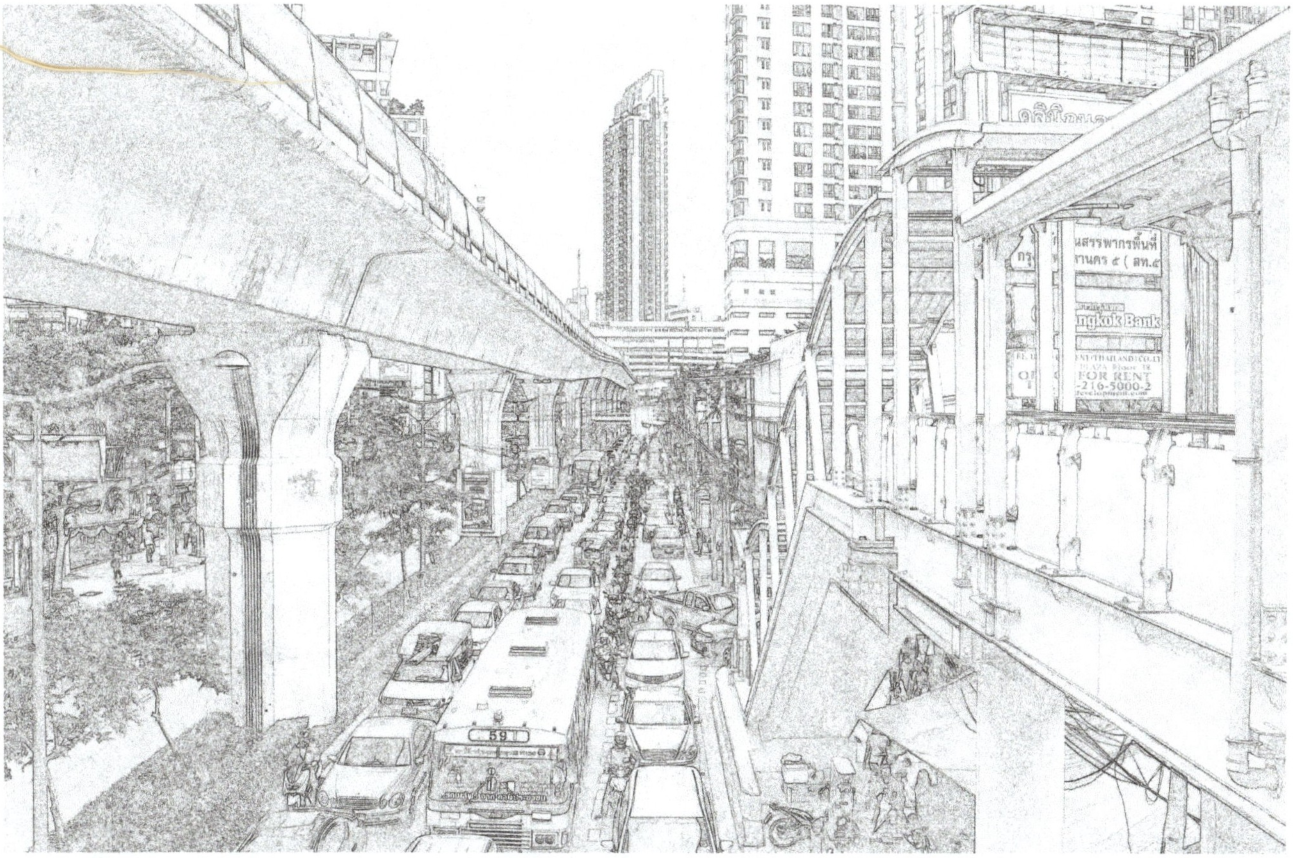

Uncle JOHN

CITY and CHURCH in THE OLD TOWE COLORING BOOK FOR ADULTS SKETCH DESIGN

Copyright: Published in the United States by Uncle JOHN
Published April 2017

All rights reserved. No part of this publication may be reproduced, stored in retrieval system, copied in any form or by any means, electronic, mechanical, photocopying, recording or otherwise transmitted without written permission from the publisher. Please do not participate in or encourage piracy of this material in any way. You must not circulate this book in any format. Uncle Johne *does not control or direct users' actions and is not responsible for the information or content shared, harm and/or actions of the book readers.*

ISBN-13 : 978-1545420188

ISBN-10 : 1545420181

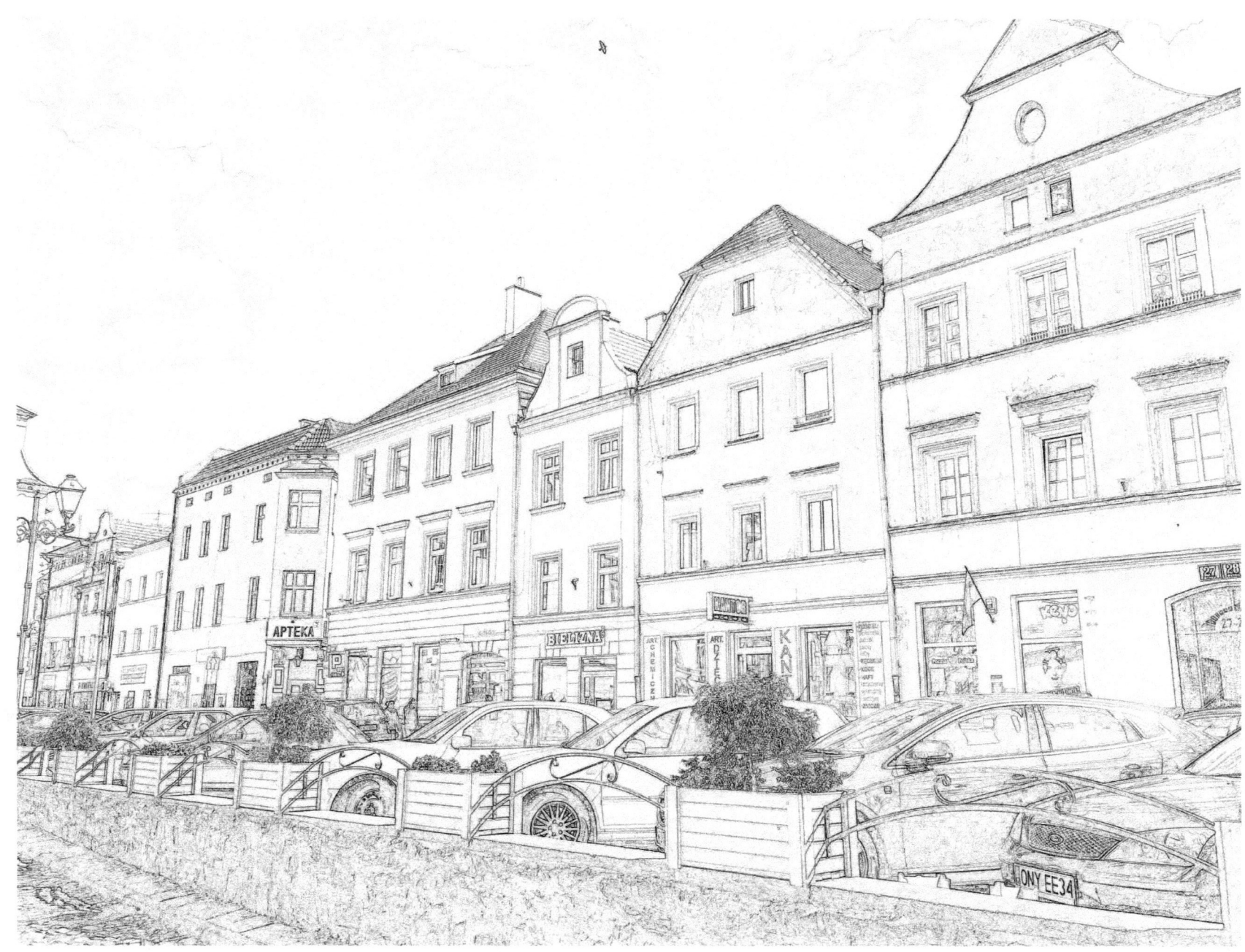

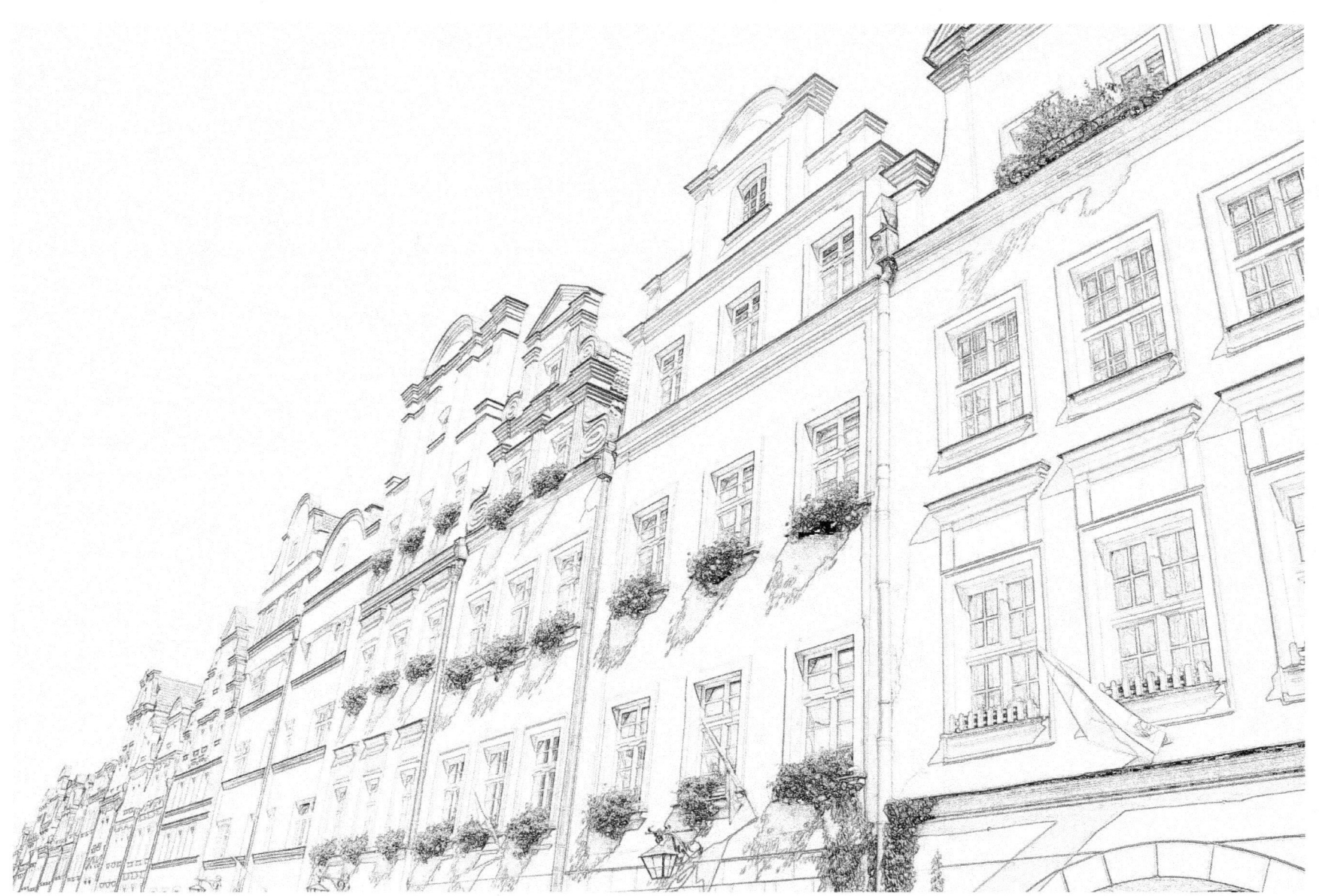

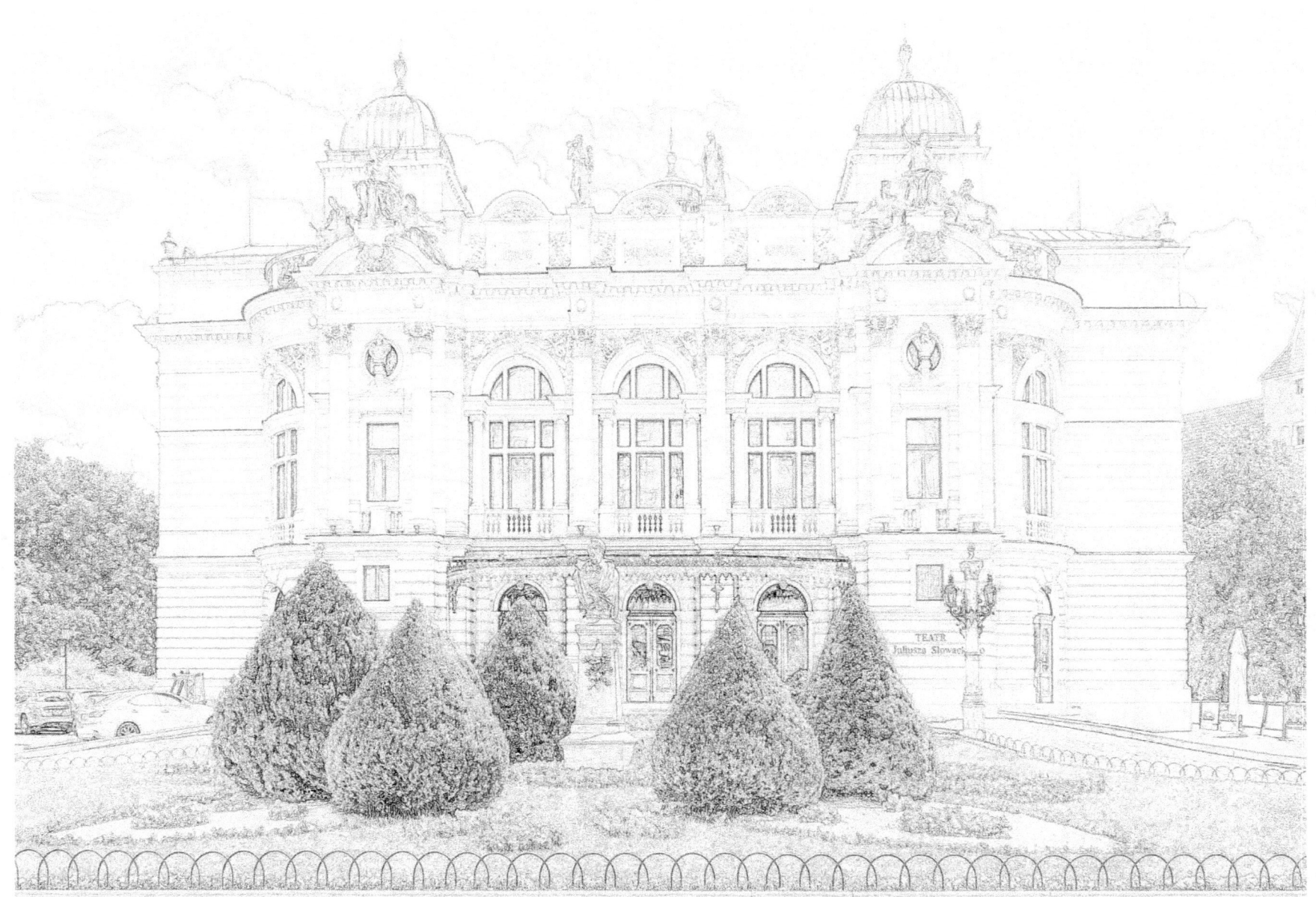

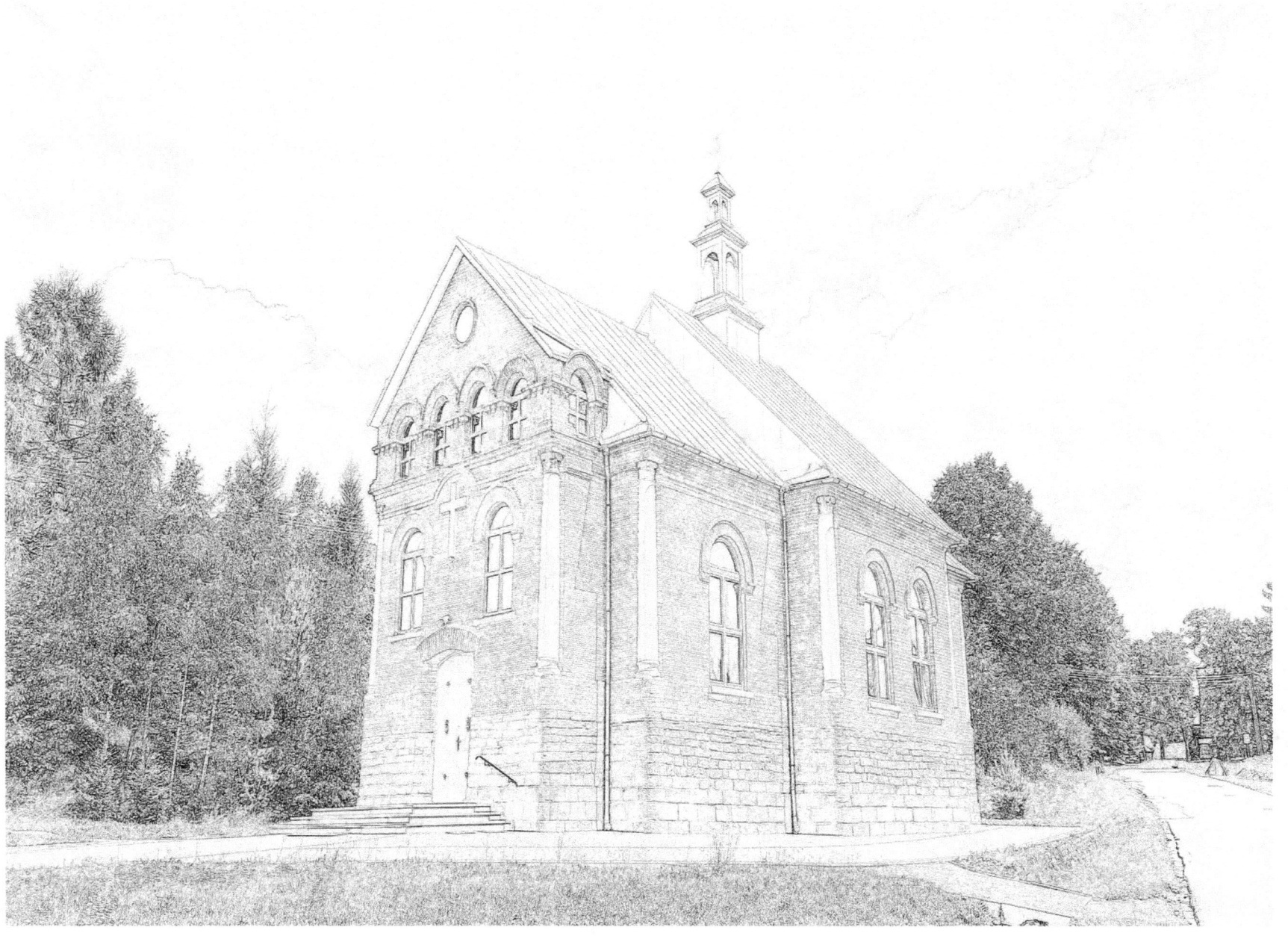

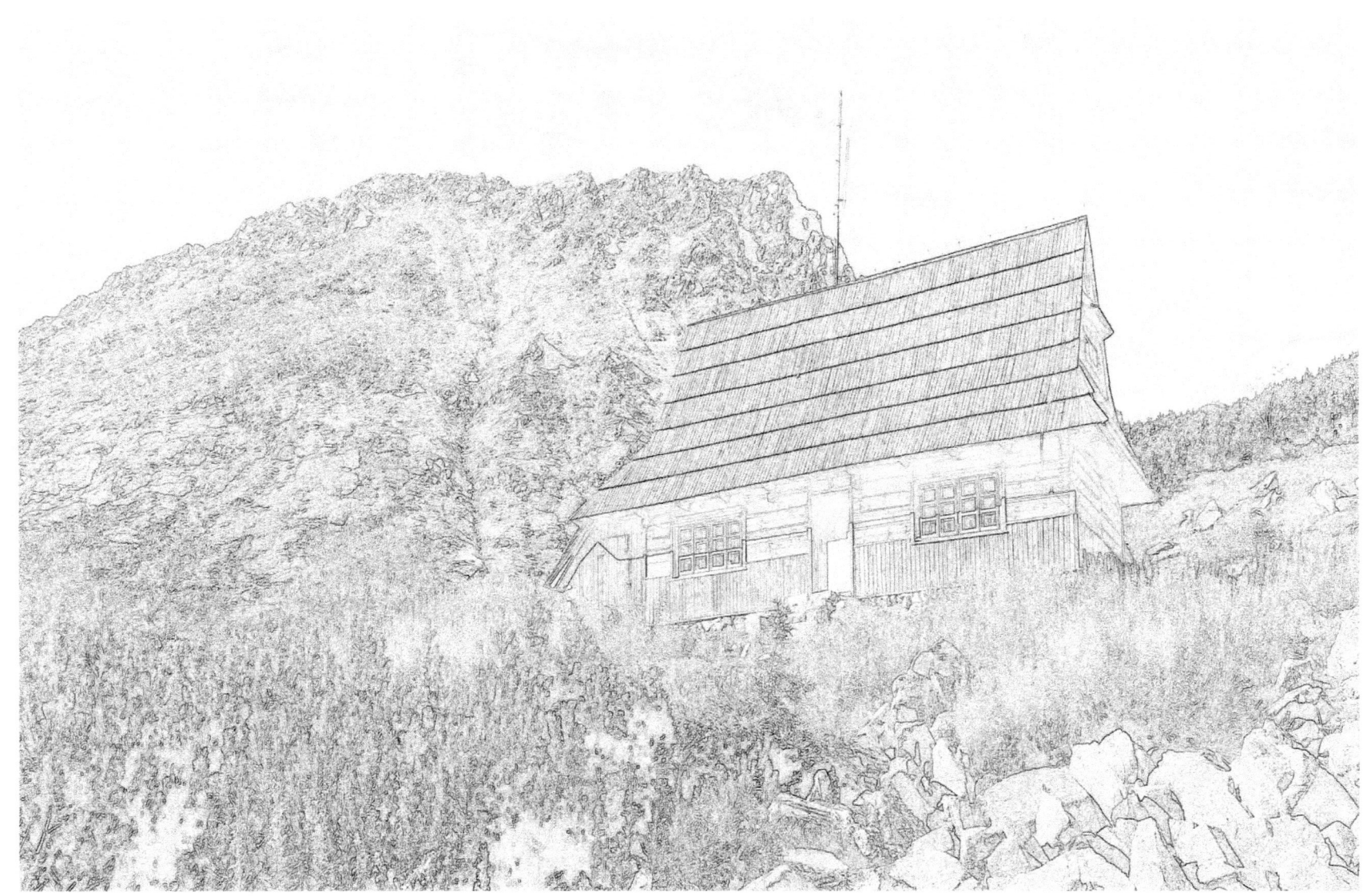

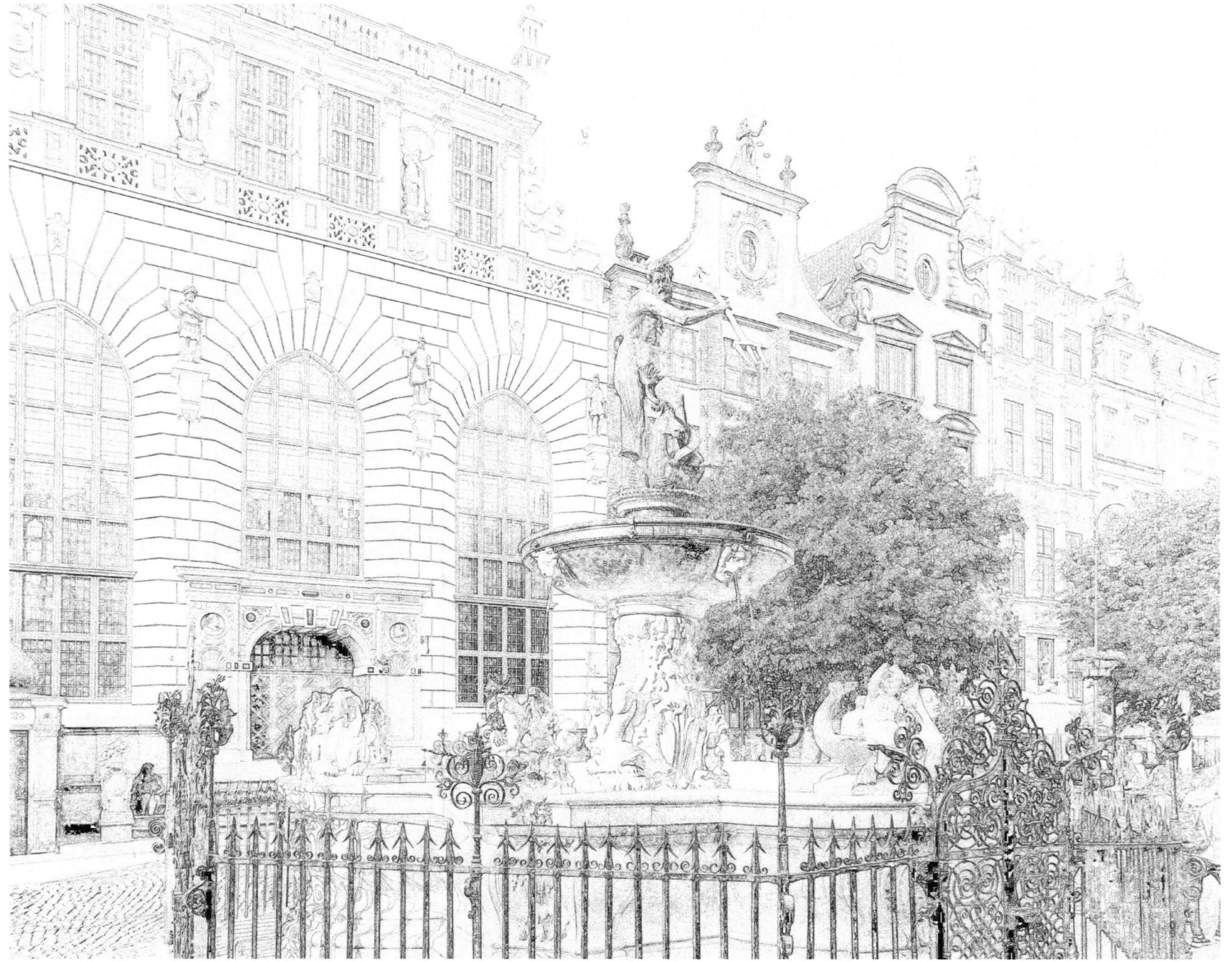

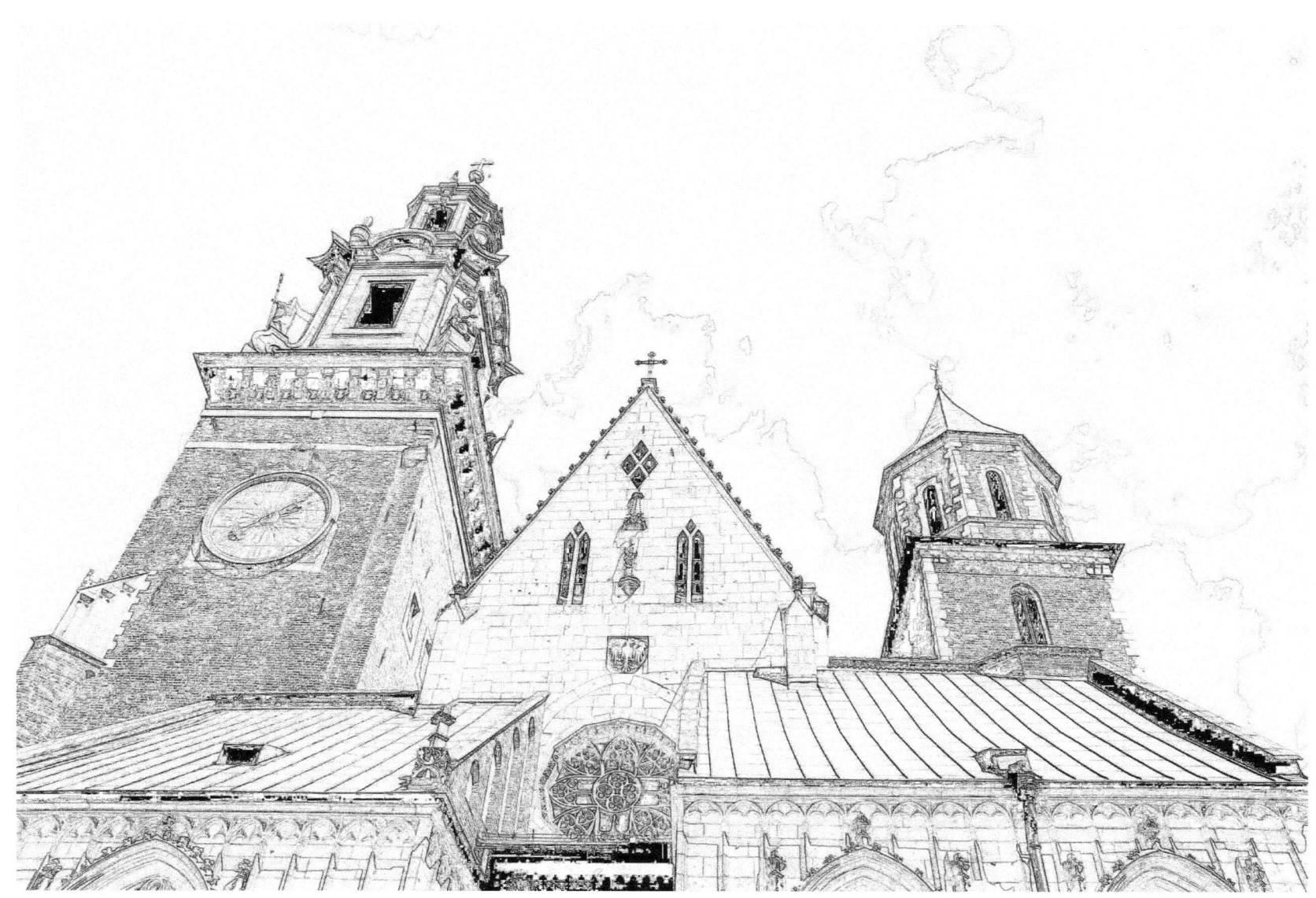

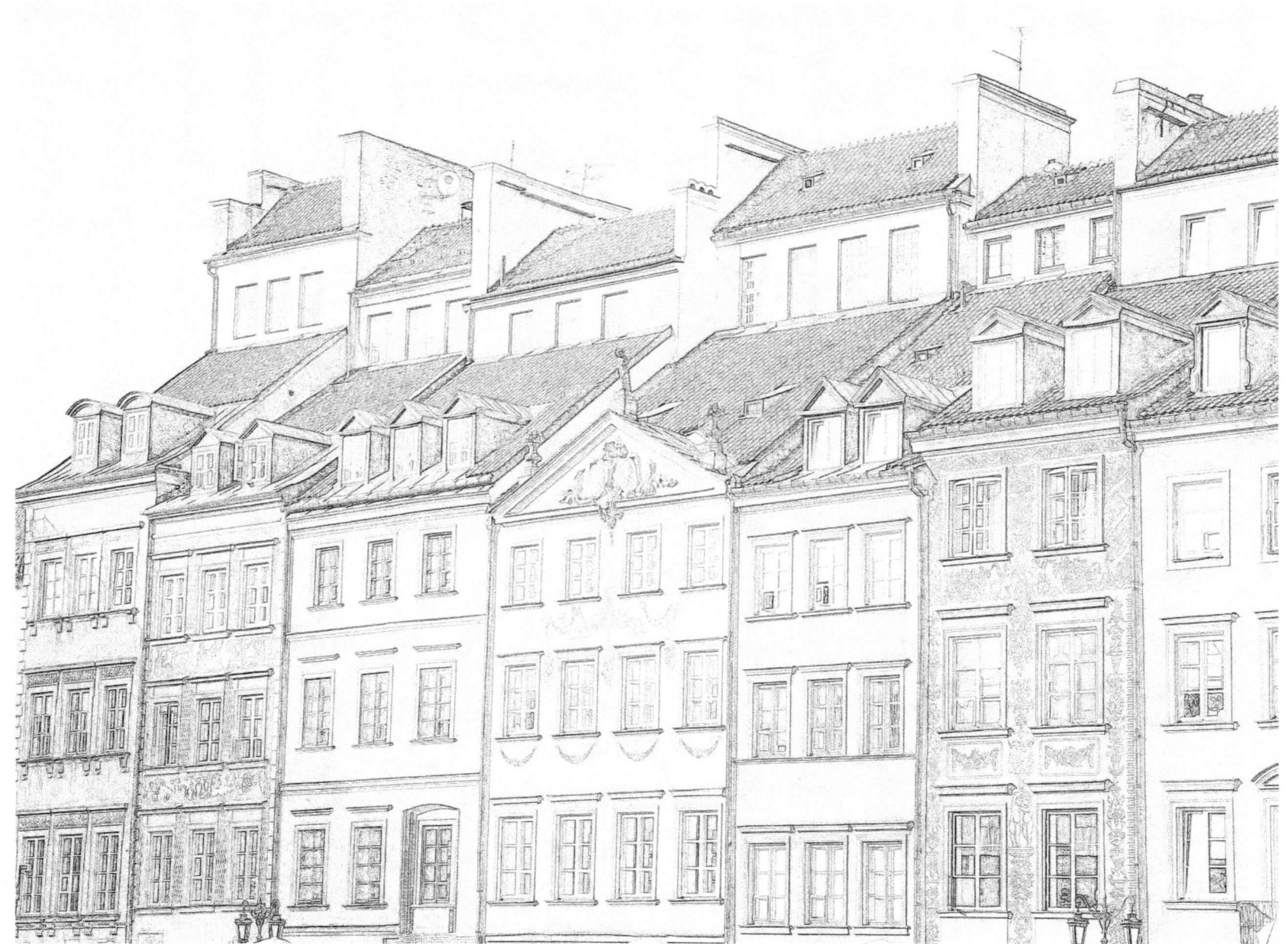

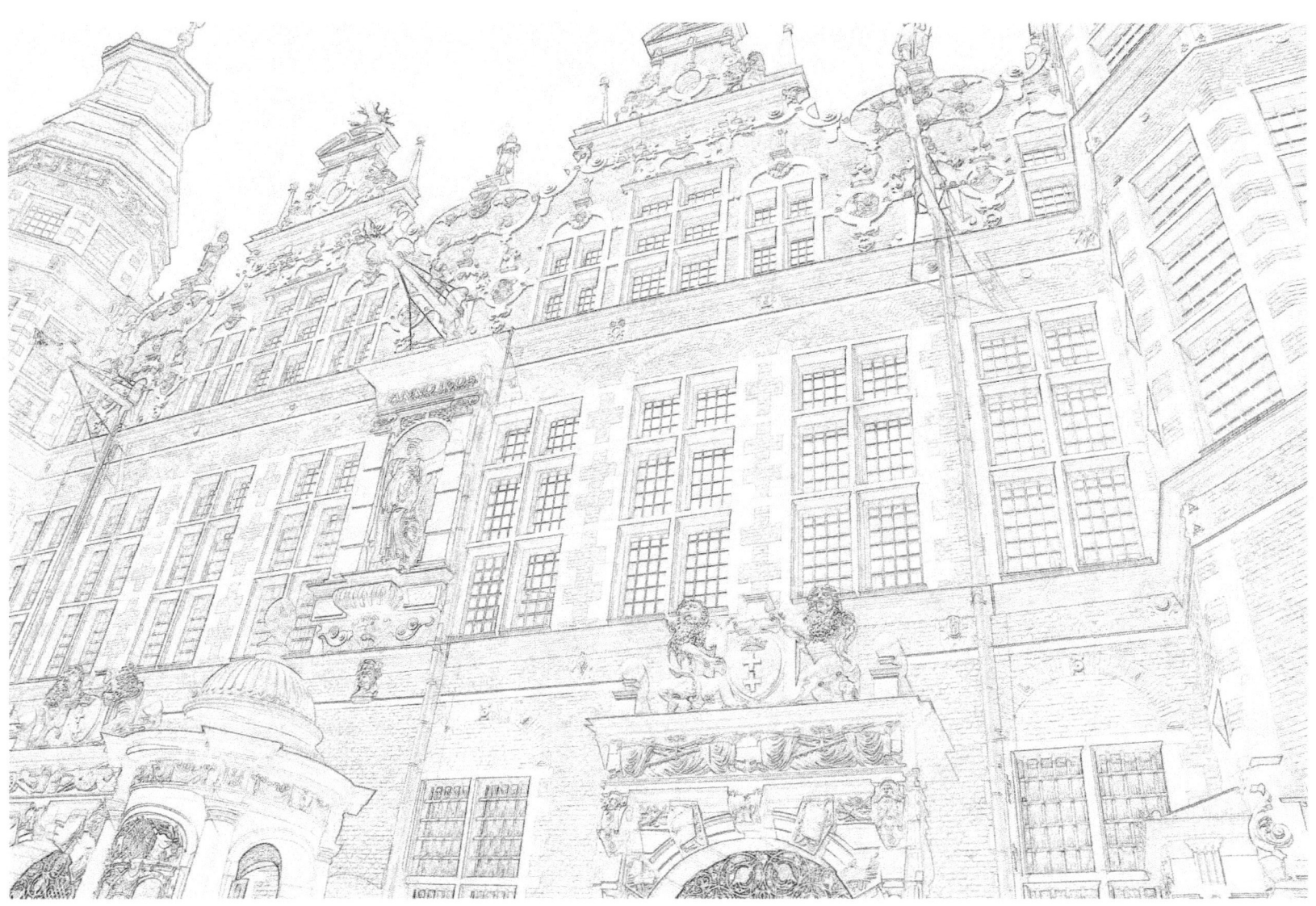

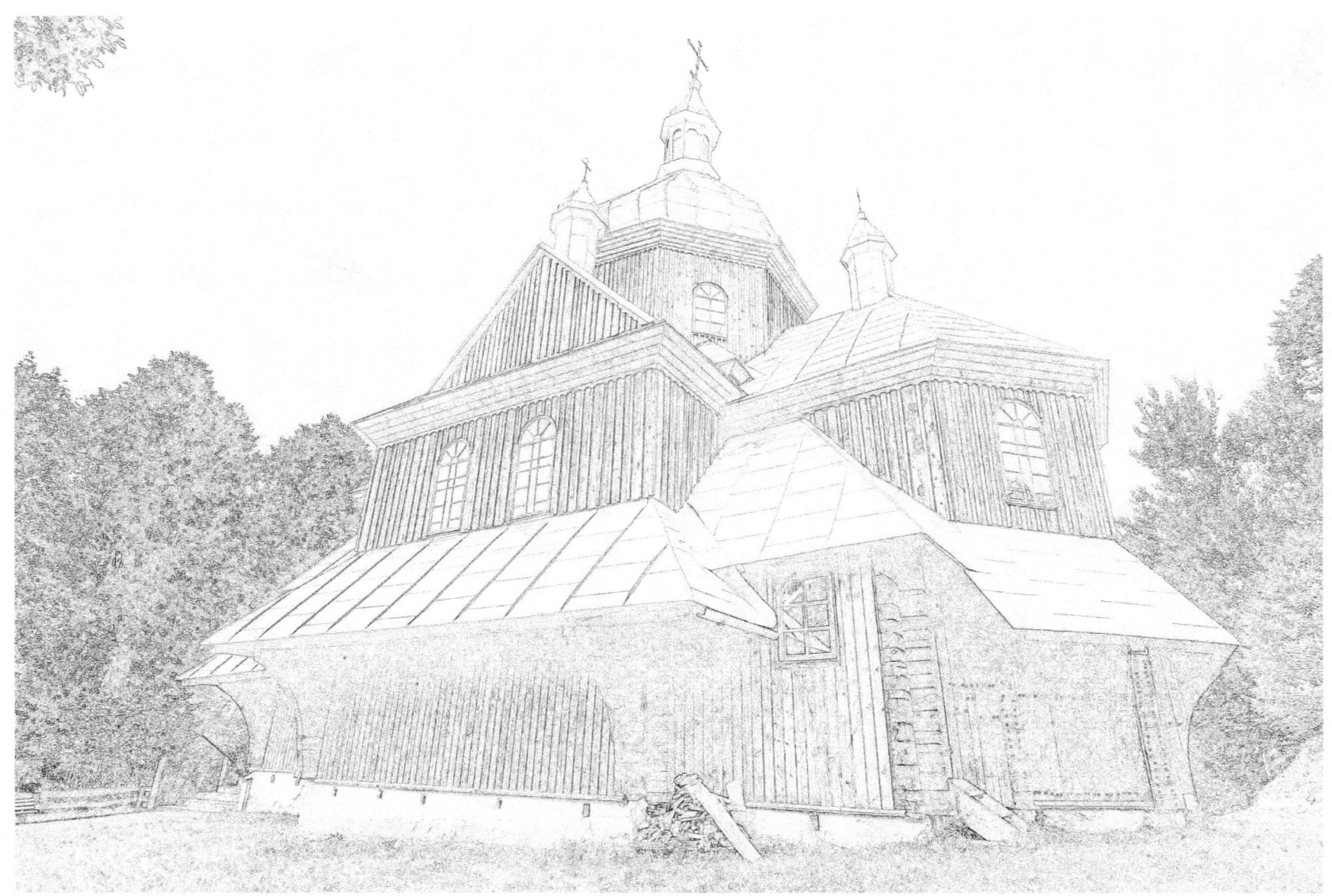

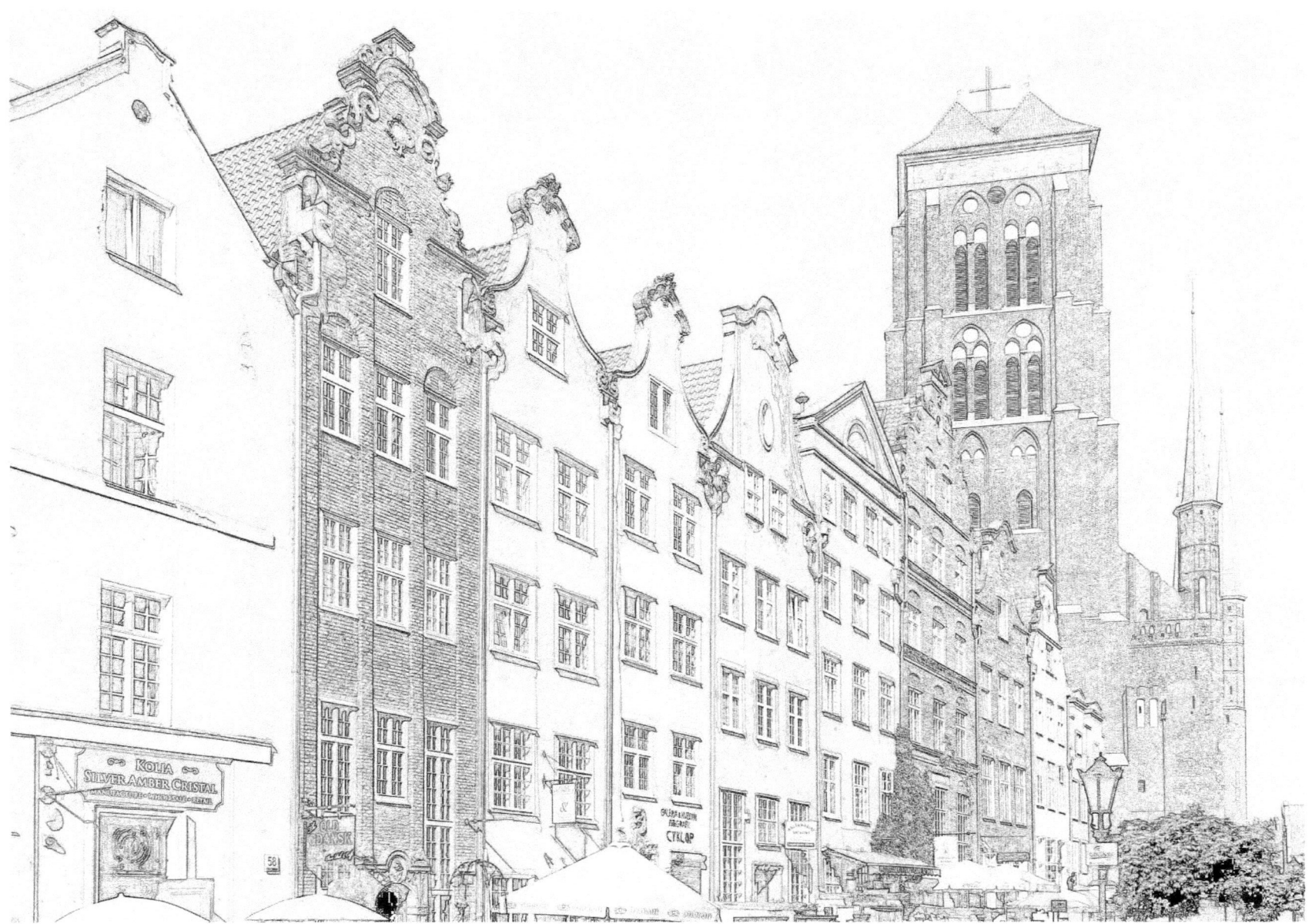

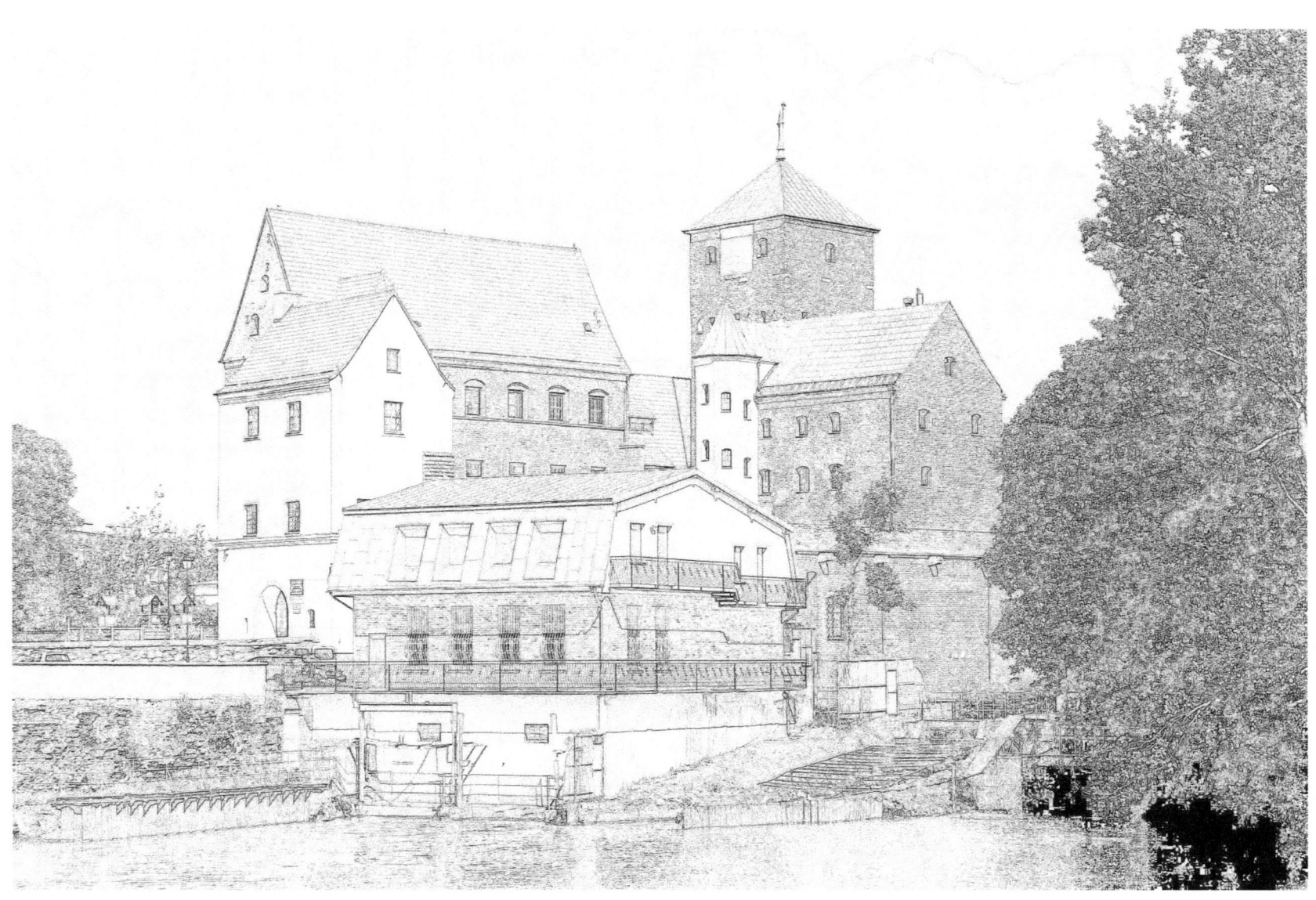

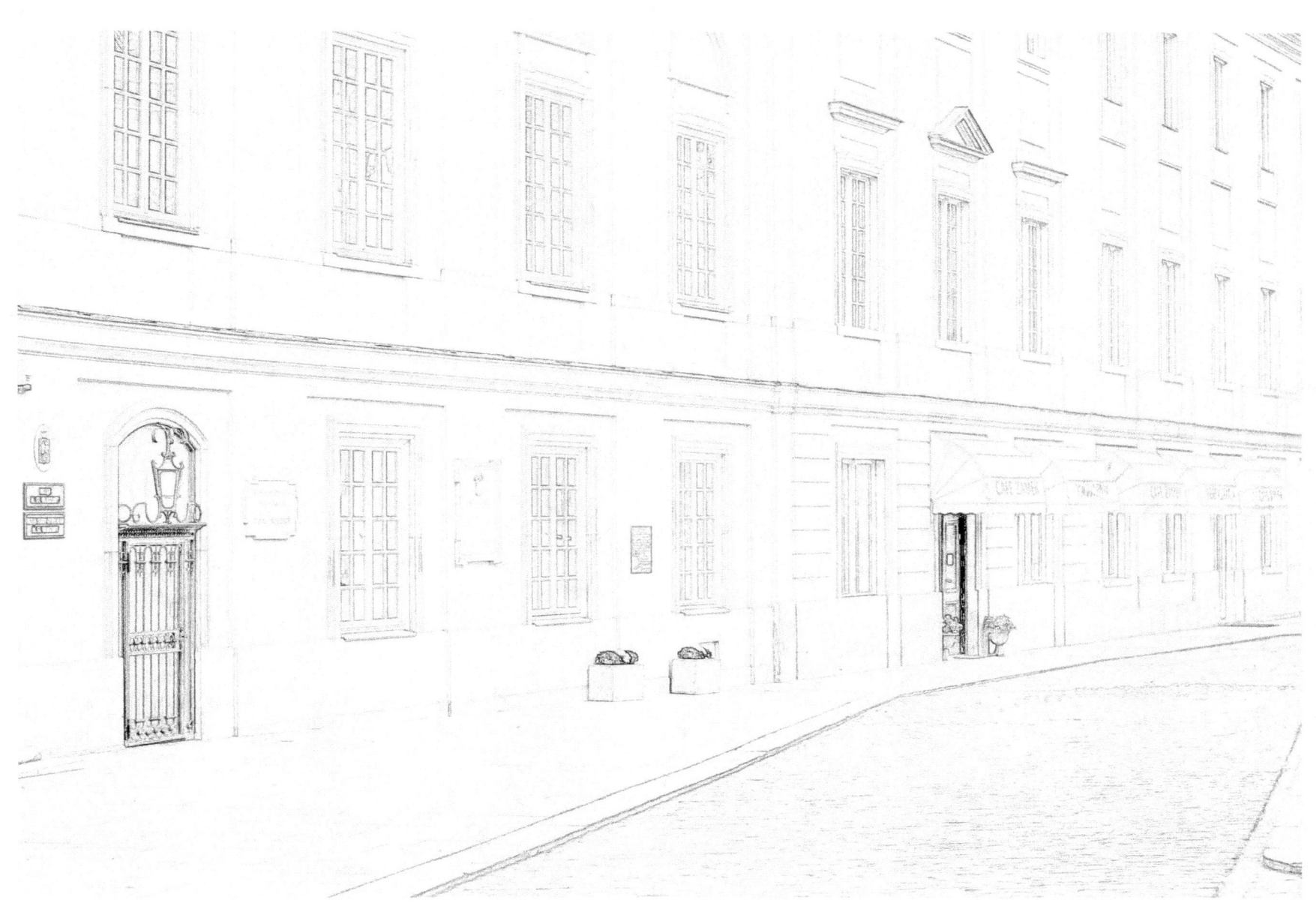

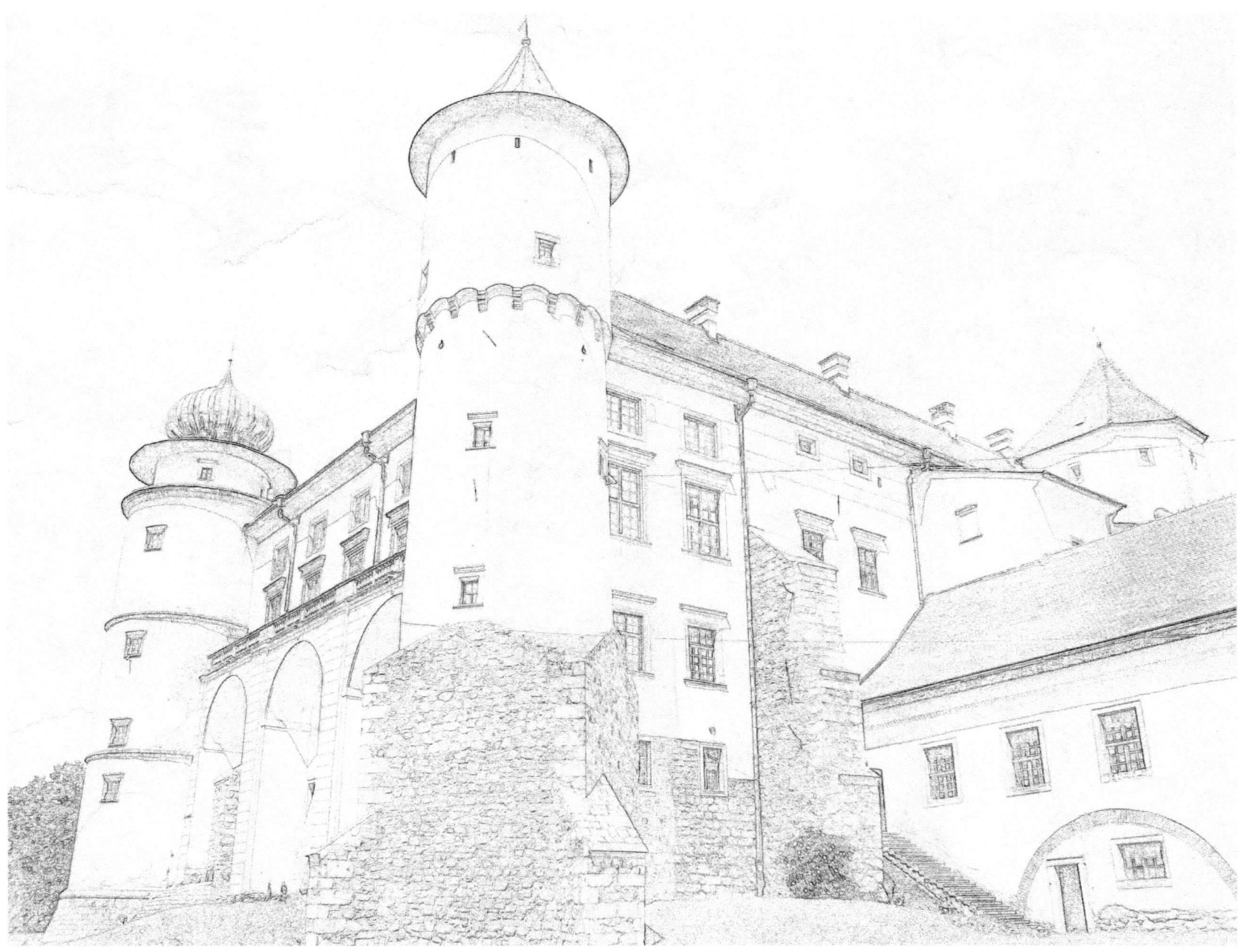

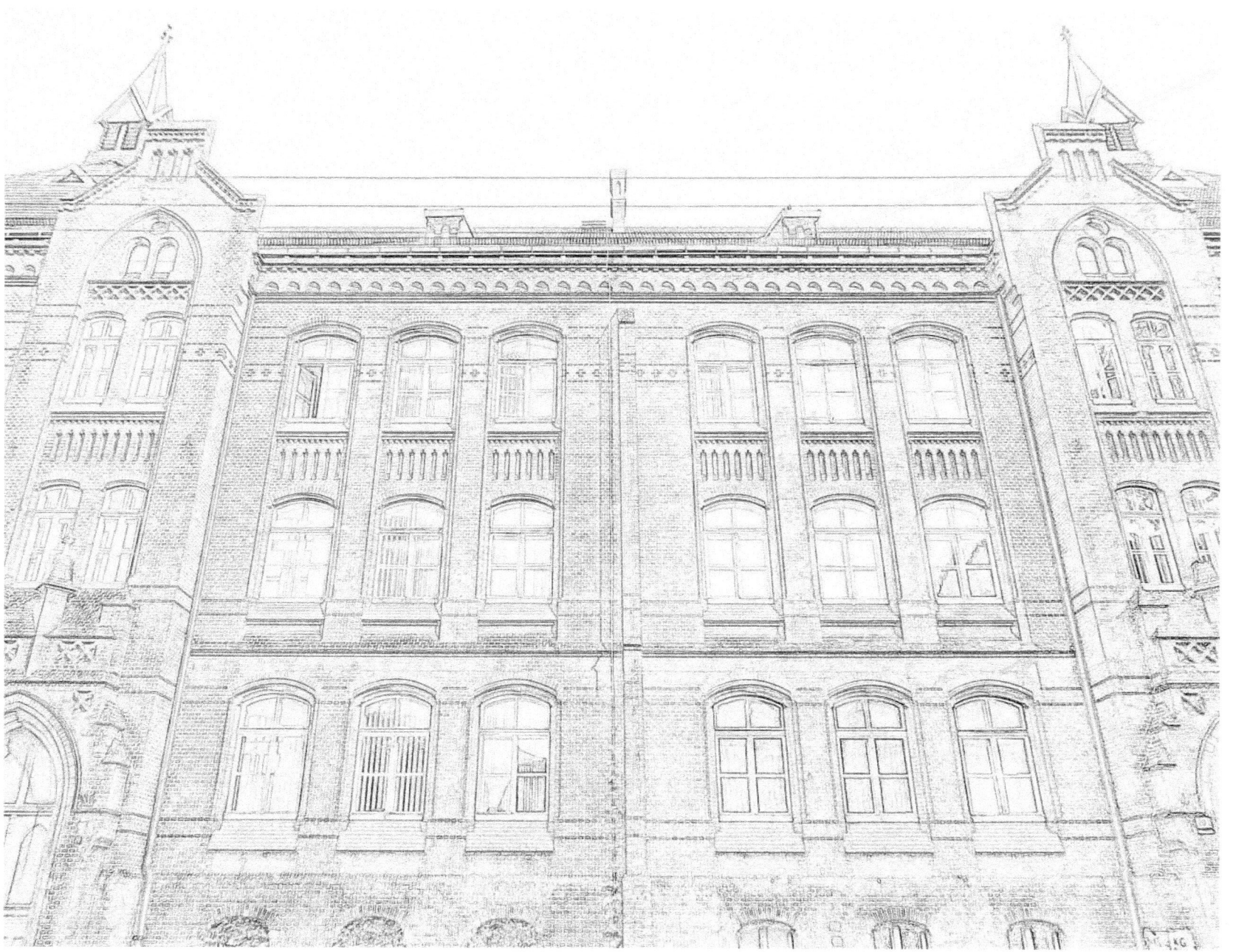

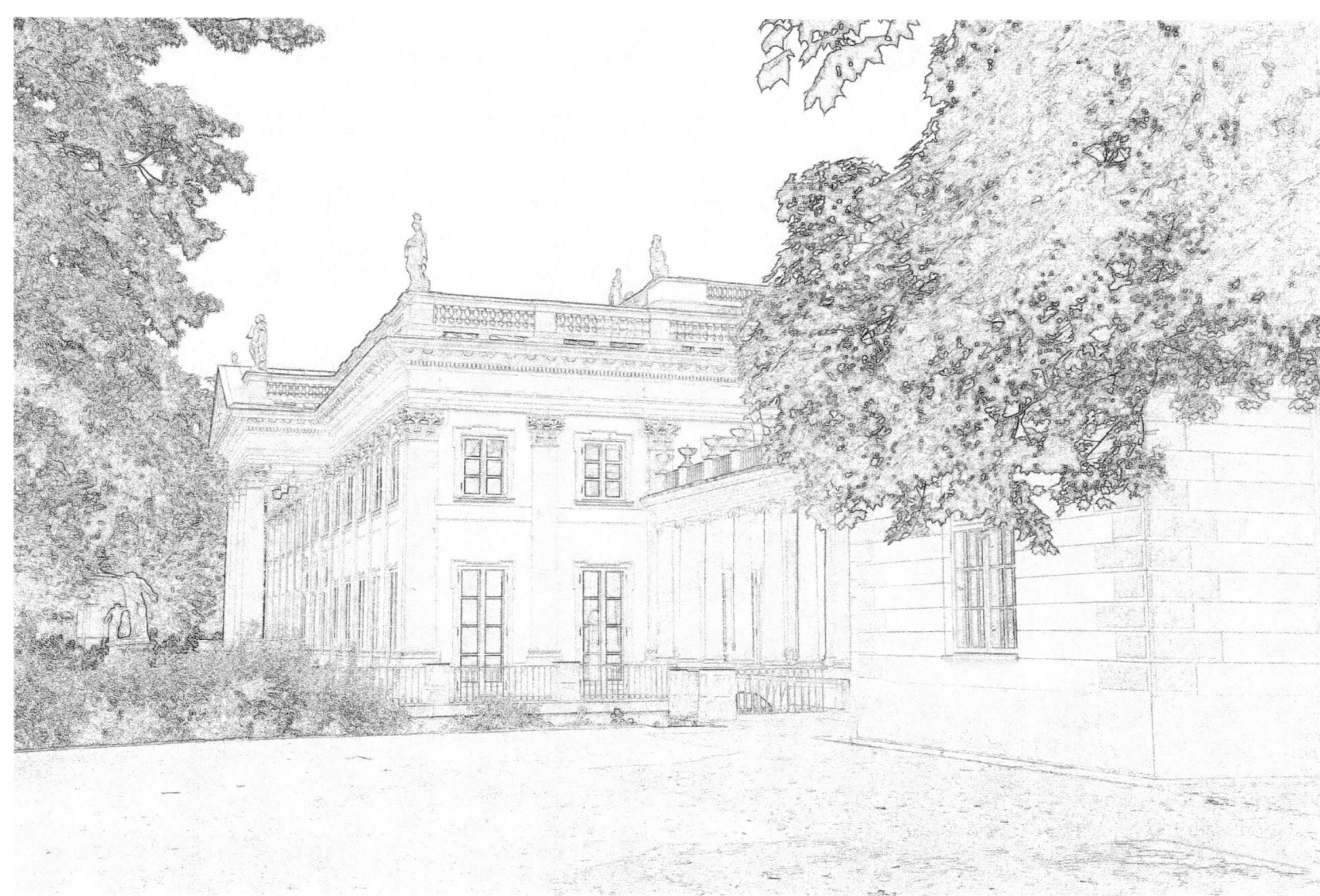

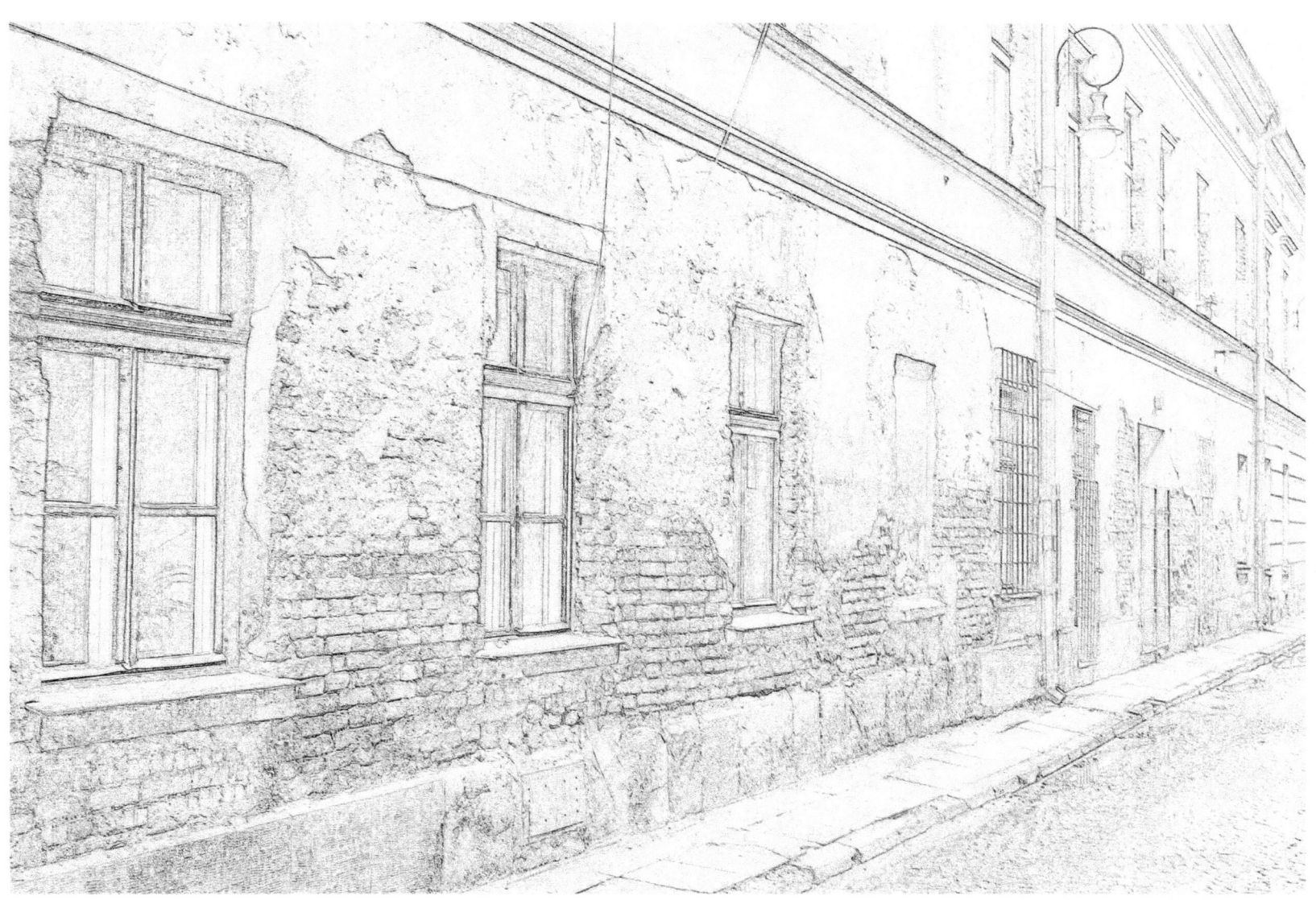

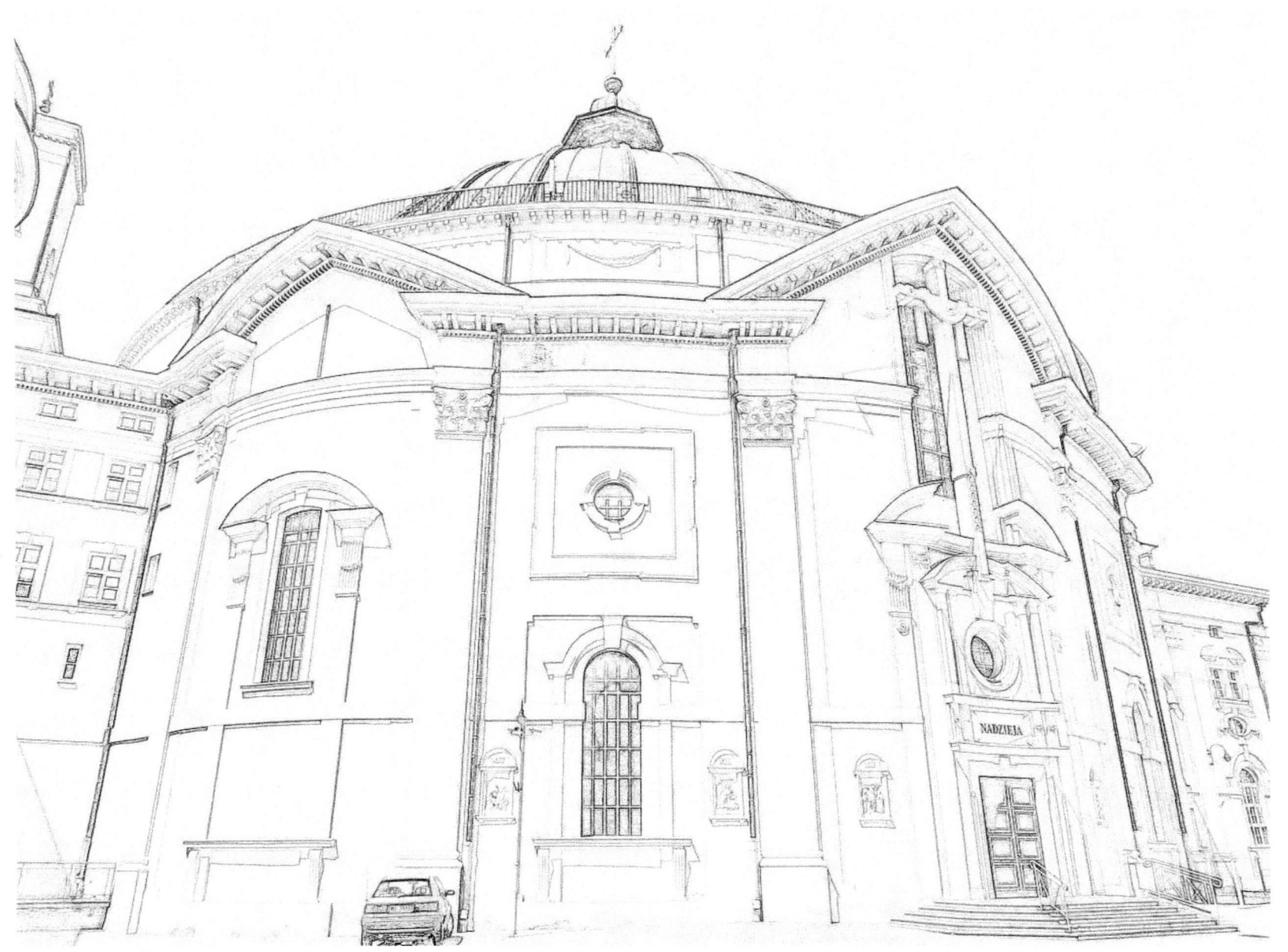

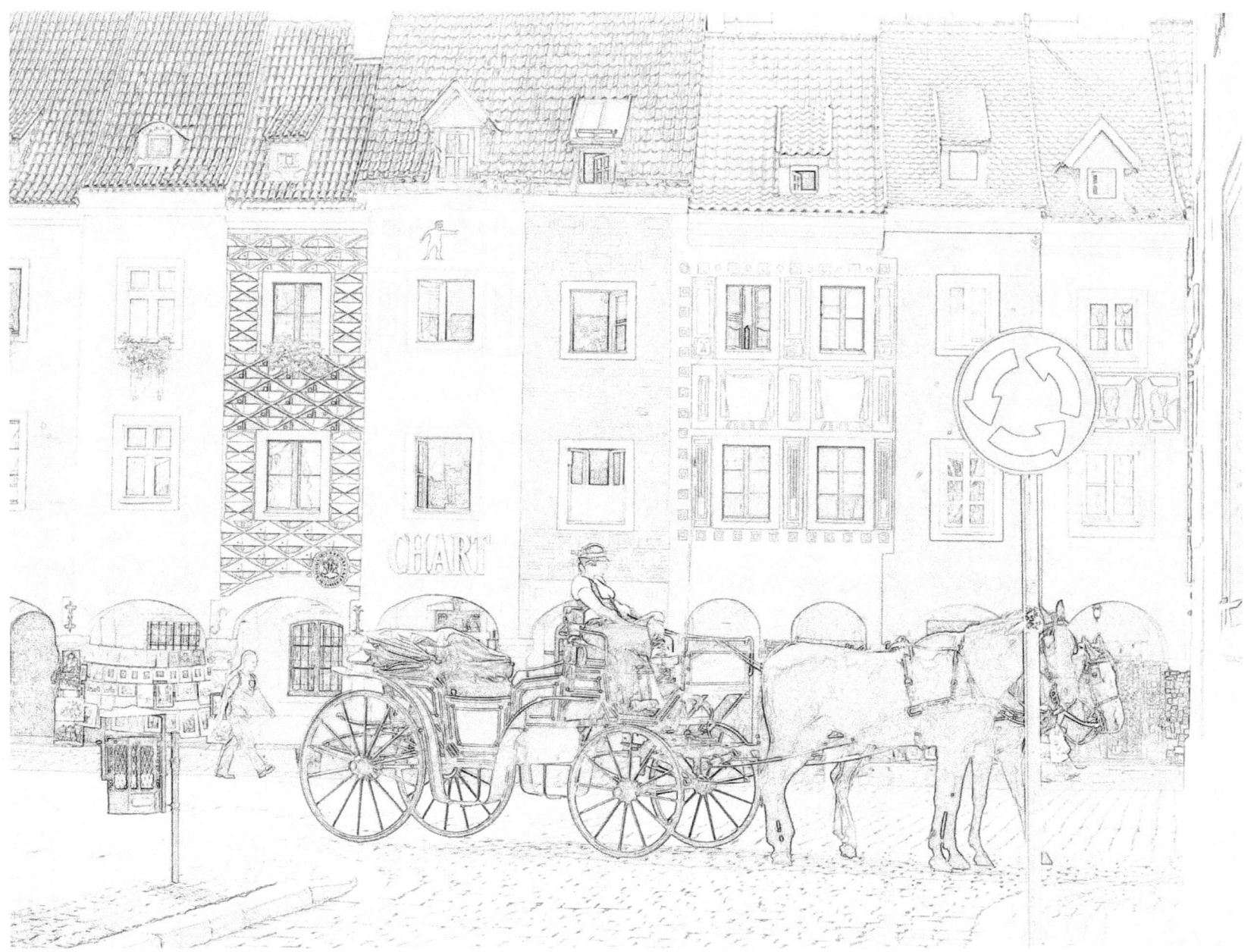

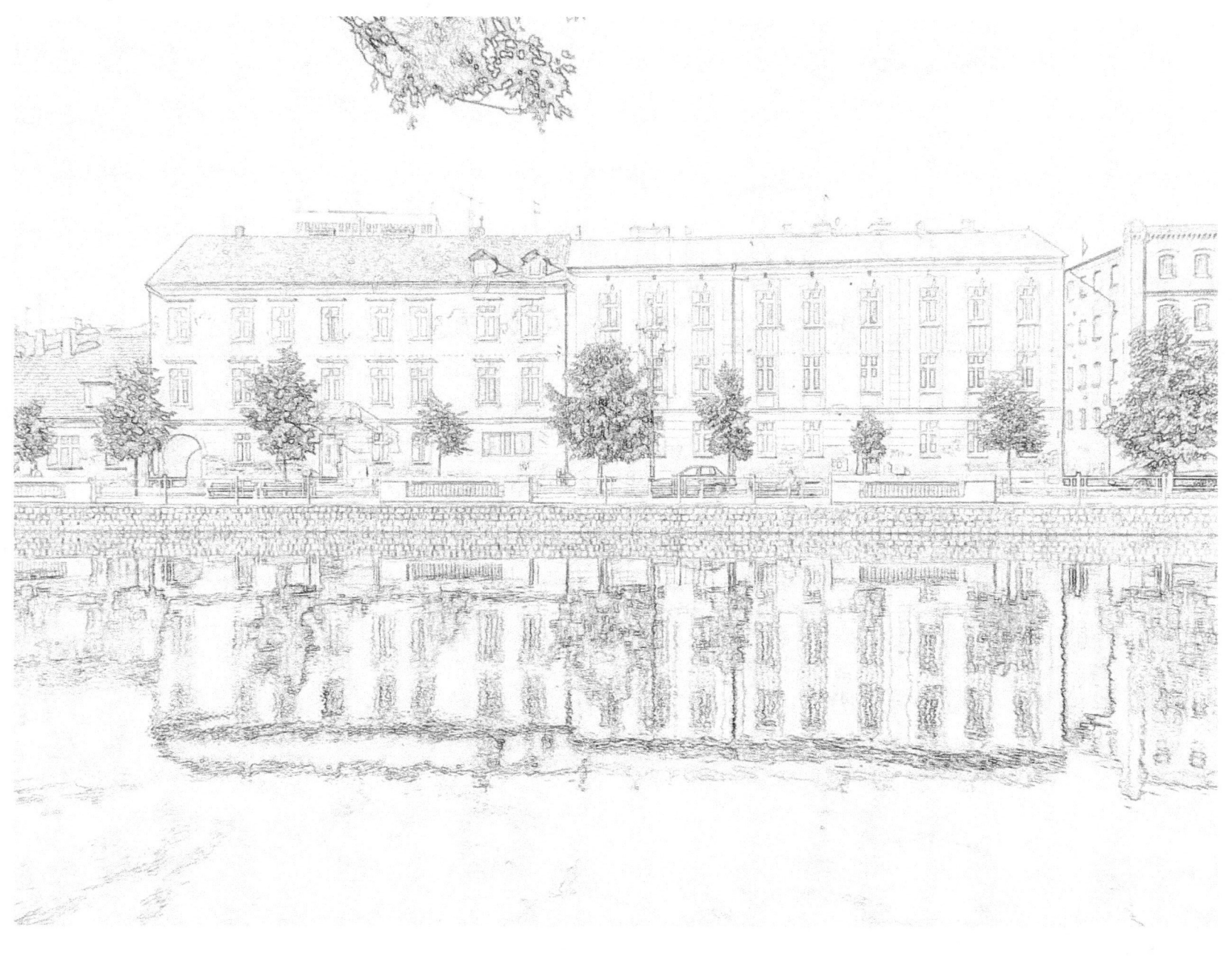

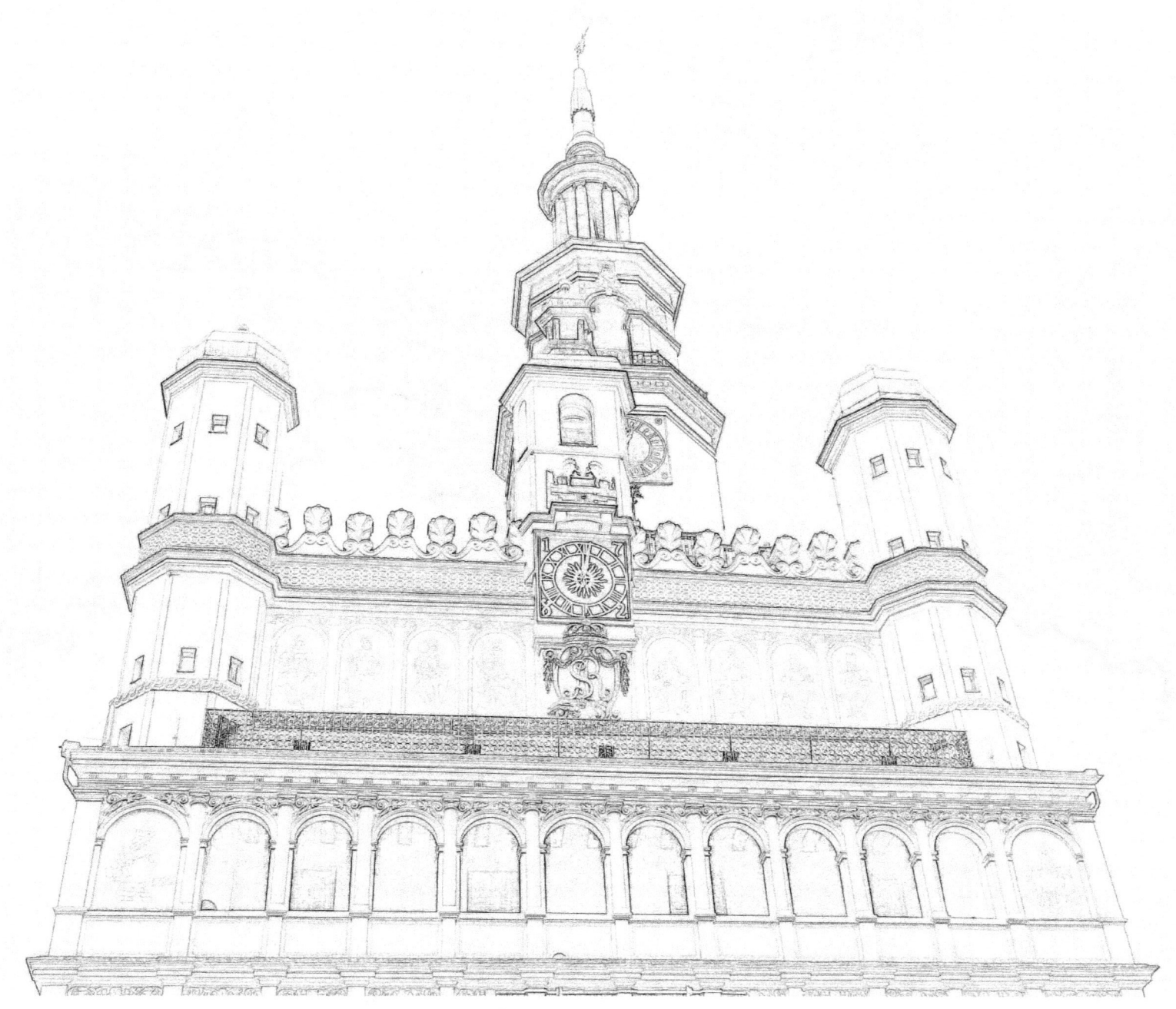

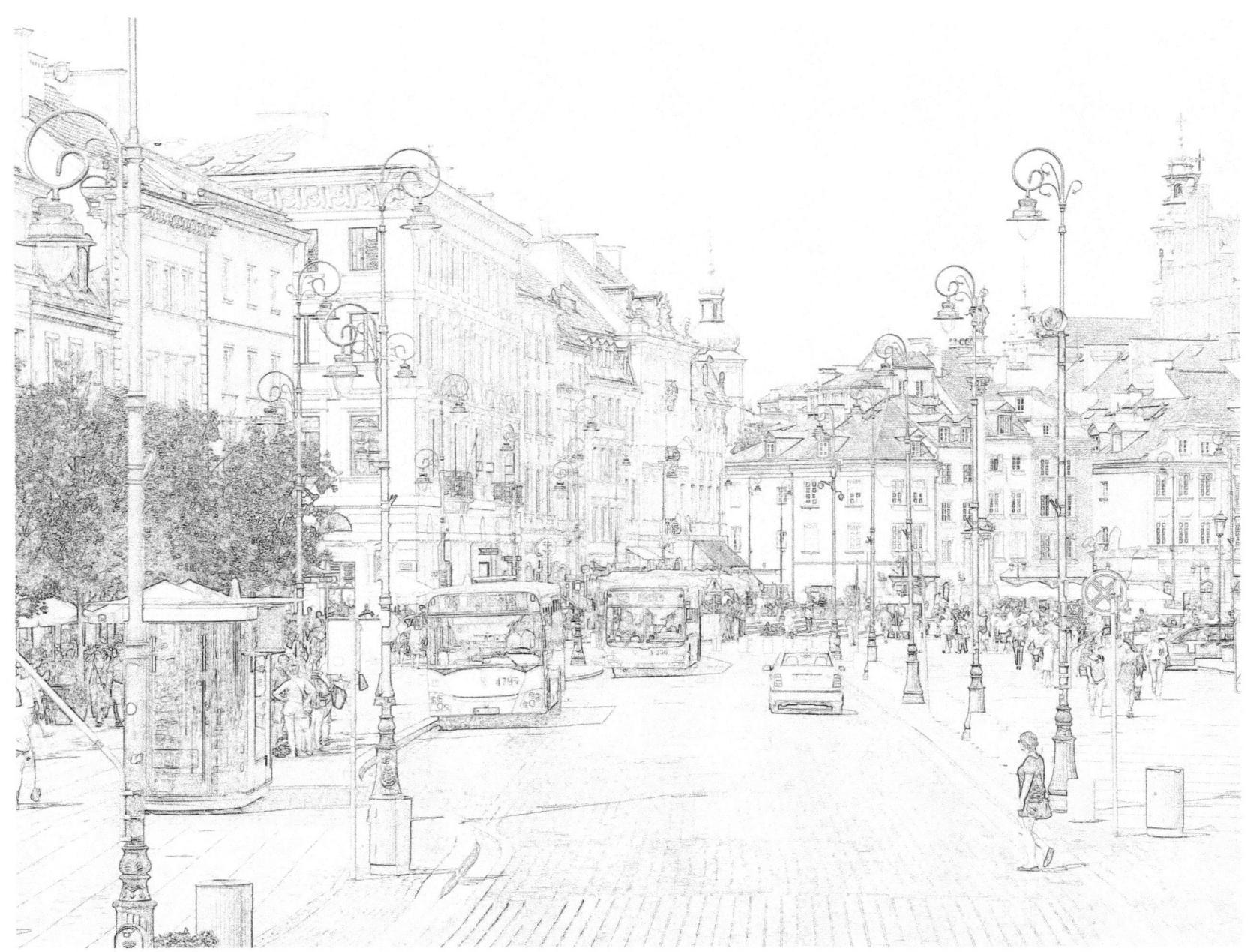

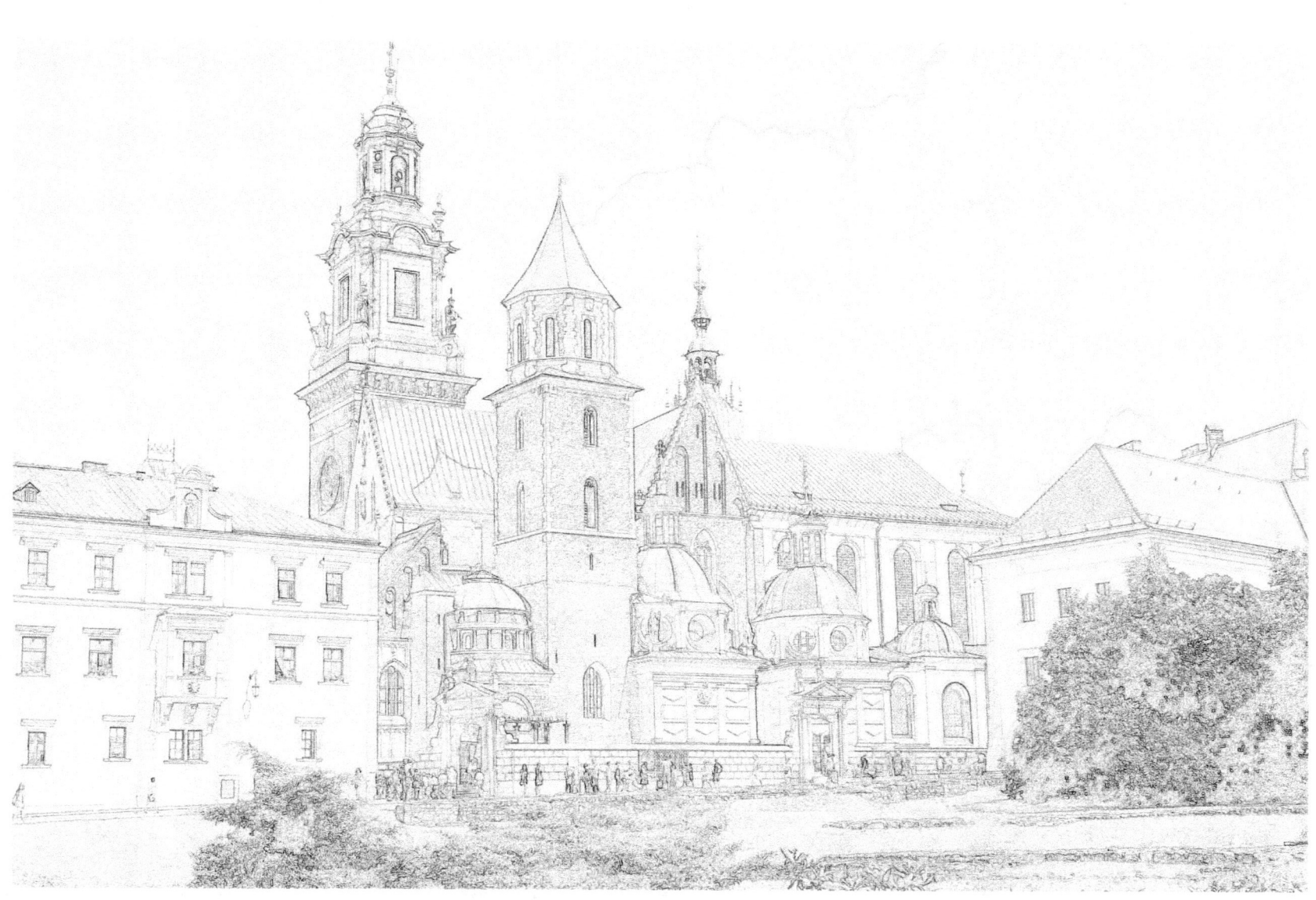

Thank you

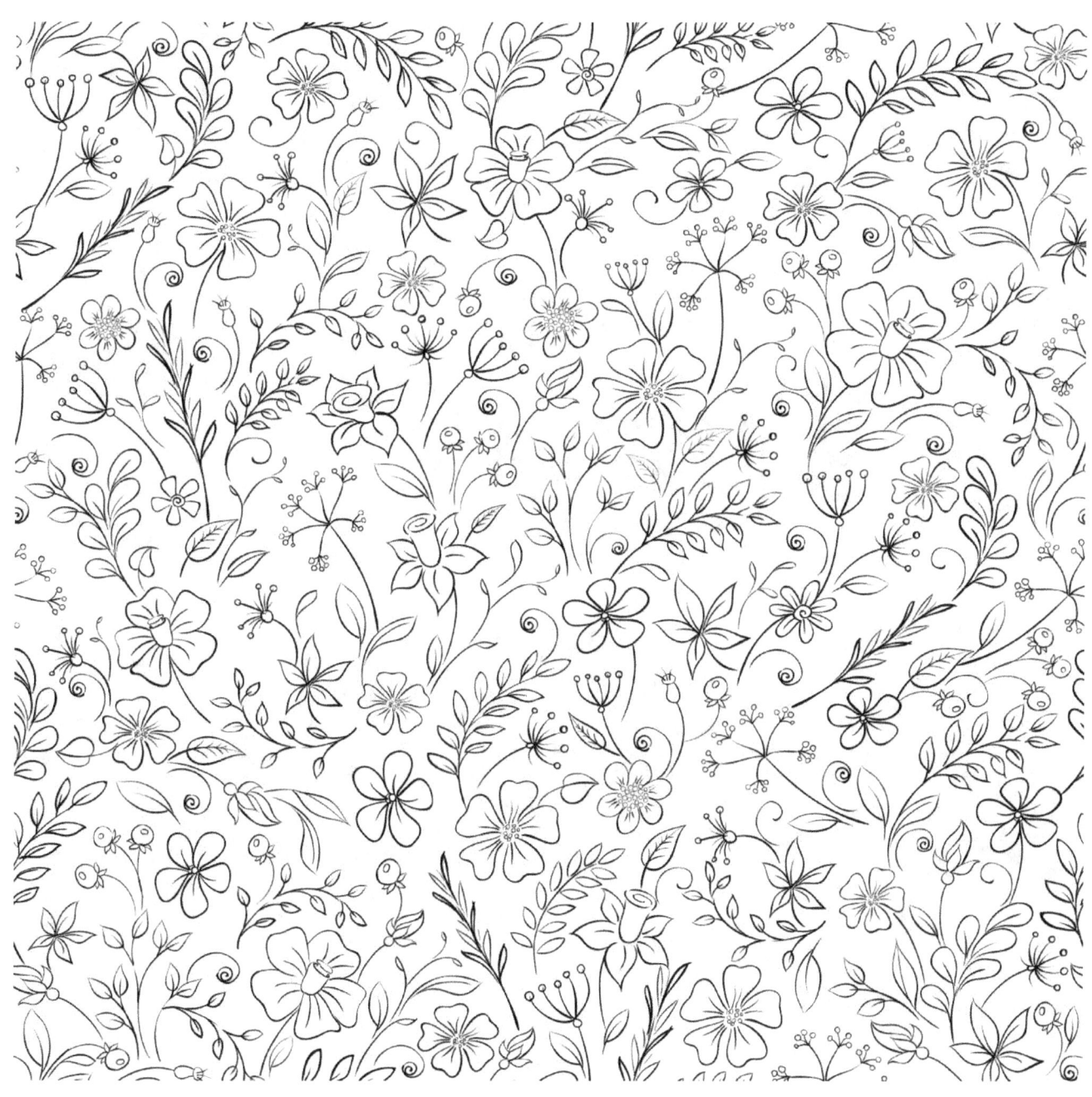

www.ingramcontent.com/pod-product-compliance
Lightning Source LLC
Chambersburg PA
CBHW081125180526
45170CB00008B/3011